LEWIS and CLARK'S
Voyage of Discovery

James P. Burger

The Rosen Publishing Group's
PowerKids Press™
New York

For Aggie, a loving, adventurous, and sorely missed companion

Published in 2002 by The Rosen Publishing Group, Inc.
29 East 21st Street, New York, NY 10010

First Edition

Book Design: Emily Muschinske

Project Editor: Kathy Campbell

Photo Credits: title page © Dean Cornwell/Montana State Historical Society; pp. 4, 5 (right) © Dick Durrance/National Geographic Society; pp. 5 (left), 8, 9 (lower left), 13 (coin), 17 (inset) 18 (explorer), 21(medicine man), 23 © The Granger Collection; pp. 6, 13 (village) © North Wind Picture Archives; pp. 9 (book, clock), 10 (peace medal), 14 (gun, compass, map) © National Geographic; p. 9 (map) © Emily Muschinske; pp. 10, (top), 17 (meeting Shoshone), © SuperStock; pp.10 (peace medal), 13 (left) Archive Photos; p. 14 (falls) © Montana State Historical Society/A.E. Matthews; pp. 18 (mountains, Fort Clatsop), 21 (right) © Archive Photos.

Background on all pages is a composite of images taken from Lewis and Clark's journals.

Burger, James P.
    Lewis and Clark's voyage of discovery / James P. Burger – 1st ed.
        p. cm. — (The library of the westward expansion)
Includes index.
    ISBN 0–8239–5848–5
1. Lewis and Clark Expedition (1804–1806)—Juvenile literature. 2. West (U.S.)—Discovery and exploration—Juvenile literature. 3. West (U.S.)—Discovery and travel—Juvenile literature. [1. Lewis and Clark Expedition (1804–1806) 2. Lewis, Meriwether, 1774–1809. 3. Clark, William, 1770–1838. 4. Explorers. 5. West (U.S.)—Discovery and exploration.] I. Title. II. Series.
    F592.7 .B93 2001
    917.804'2—dc21

00-011391

Manufactured in the United States of America

Contents

1 A New Place to Explore 4

2 Lewis Meets Clark 7

3 Voyage into the Unknown 8

4 An Unfriendly Meeting 11

5 A Brave Woman Called Sacagawea 12

6 The Great Falls 15

7 Help from the Shoshone 16

8 Over the Mountains and to the Sea 19

9 A Risky Return 20

10 Welcomed Heroes 22

Glossary 23

Index 24

Web Sites 24

A New Place to Explore

The United States was much smaller in size before 1800. Only Native Americans and a small number of French and Spanish people lived west of the Mississippi River. In 1803, President Thomas Jefferson doubled the country's size. He bought the Louisiana **Territory** from France. Today the area of the Louisiana Purchase is **divided** into the 15 states that lie between the Mississippi River and the Rocky Mountains.

In 1804, Jefferson sent an **expedition** led by two brave men, Meriwether Lewis and William Clark, to find a water route to the Pacific Ocean. He told them to **explore** the land and to take notes about everything they saw and did along the way. He wanted them to study the plants and animals. Jefferson told them to describe the Native Americans they met and to become their friends.

Before Meriwether Lewis (right) and William Clark went on the Voyage of Discovery, they had to learn all about animals, plants, and fossils. Lewis had a keelboat made for the trip (far right). This drawing is what it might have looked like. Clark drew this picture of a "cock of the plains" (above) during the trip.

Lewis Meets Clark

Meriwether Lewis was born on August 18, 1774, near Charlottesville, Virginia. Growing up, Lewis became interested in nature and learned how to use plants to treat illnesses. When he was 20, Lewis joined the **militia**.

William Clark was born in Caroline County, Virginia, on August 1, 1770. When he was 15, Clark and his family moved to the Kentucky **frontier**, in the valley of the Ohio River. At the age of 19, he joined the military and quickly became a captain. Clark first met Lewis when they served together along the Ohio River. They soon became friends.

Lewis (top) and Clark (bottom) first met in the Ohio River Valley (background). In 1801, Lewis worked as President Jefferson's assistant. Jefferson (center) chose Lewis to lead an expedition into the American West. Lewis asked Clark to share the command.

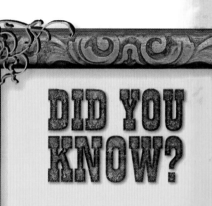

DID YOU KNOW?

Lewis had a special boat built for the trip west. It was a keelboat, which had a flat bottom so it could float in shallow water. He named it *Discovery*. It took 22 men to row the boat, which had a cannon.

7

Voyage into the Unknown

On May 14, 1804, the Voyage of Discovery began. Lewis and Clark entered the Missouri River near St. Louis. With about 50 men and Lewis's dog, Seaman, they **trekked** into unfamiliar territories. Clark made maps of their route. Lewis wrote about the Native American people they met. He also carefully described the plants and animals that the men **encountered**. By the end of August, they reached the prairies of Kansas, Nebraska, and Iowa. On the high plains of South Dakota, they found small animals that looked almost like squirrels, except for their short tails. These brown, furry animals sat upright on top of their **burrows** and barked. The men named the creatures prairie dogs because they barked like dogs.

Top: Grizzly bears were among the animals that Lewis and Clark saw on their trip.

Right, clockwise: Lewis carried this English-made watch on the journey; this is Clark's elk-skin bound journal, or notebook; the men gave this animal, a prairie dog, its name; a map shows the route that the men took on the voyage.

WASHINGTON

Fort
Clatsop

Camp
Disappointment

Great
Falls

MISSOURI RIVER

Fort
Mandan

SNAKE

COLUMBIA RIVER

Traveller's
Rest

Three
Forks

NORTH
DAKOTA

OREGON

YELLOWSTONE RIVER

IDAHO

MONTANA

OREGON TERRITORY

ROCKY MOUNTAINS

WYOMING

SOUTH
DAKOTA

MISSOURI RIVER

IOWA

NEBRASKA

ILLINOIS

OHIO

INDIANA

OHIO RIVER

Washington, D.C.

LOUISIANA PURCHASE

St. Louis

KENTUCKY

MISSOURI

Above: *Artist Oscar Berninghaus painted this picture in 1903–06 that shows the Teton Sioux meeting Lewis and Clark and their men.*

Left: *This Jefferson Peace Medal, made of silver, shows two hands held in friendship.*

An Unfriendly Meeting

In 1804, near today's city of Pierre, South Dakota, the members of the expedition met the Teton Sioux. The Teton Sioux were not friendly to the explorers. Lewis and Clark, hoping to be accepted as friends, gave the Teton Sioux special peace medals and other gifts.

On September 25, 1804, three Teton Sioux warriors demanded trade goods from the explorers. They seized the rope that was attached to one of the boats. Clark drew his sword, and Lewis ordered the men to be ready to fight. Then Chief Black Buffalo agreed to let them continue upriver, if the Teton Sioux women and children would be able to meet the explorers before they left.

DID YOU KNOW?

President Jefferson gave Lewis and Clark Jefferson Peace Medals to hand out to powerful Native American leaders. Often a ceremony was held in which gifts were exchanged, a feast took place, and then speeches were made.

11

A Brave Woman Called Sacagawea

At the end of October 1804, Lewis and Clark reached the villages of the Mandan and Hidatsa. These Native Americans lived along the Missouri River. Lewis and Clark decided to spend the winter with them, near what is now Bismarck, North Dakota. They built a fort and called it Fort Mandan.

Several years before, the Hidatsa had captured a young girl named Sacagawea. Her people, the Shoshone, lived to the west, in the Rocky Mountains. She stayed with the Hidatsa and married a French Canadian fur trapper named Toussaint Charbonneau. On February 11, 1805, Sacagawea gave birth to a son and named him Jean Baptiste. She became a key member of the expedition. Sacagawea spoke the language of the Shoshone and could **interpret** for the explorers.

Top right: *This U.S. dollar from 2000 shows Sacagawea and Jean Baptiste.*

Left: *Sacagawea could speak with the Shoshone to help the explorers buy horses for the trip.*

Bottom right: *Here is a view of a Mandan village in the 1800s.*

Top: *This rifle was carried by one of the explorers during the journey.*

Right: *An explorer's compass helped show directions because its magnetic needle pointed north.*

Left: *Clark made this map of the Great Falls.*

The Great Falls

The Mandan told Lewis and Clark to expect a large waterfall on their trip. In early June 1805, the explorers came to a place where the Missouri River forked. They separated to explore both the north and the south branches. Back together a week later, they decided that the correct route headed south. They went south, and soon heard a loud rumbling. They saw thick mist rising like smoke from the river ahead. The Great Falls were much wider and higher than they had imagined. There were five waterfalls instead of one! The explorers had to carry their boats and supplies 18 miles (29 km) over land to get around the falls.

Bottom Left: *A. E. Matthews painted this view of the Great Falls.*

DID YOU KNOW?

When the explorers had to carry their boats around the falls, they got very tired. They often would fall to the ground, asleep! They met terrible storms and a flash flood almost killed them.

Help from the Shoshone

Nearing the Rocky Mountains, Lewis and Clark began to worry. They had not met the Shoshone and still had no horses. On August 8, 1805, Sacagawea pointed to a large hill. She called it The Beaver's Head because of its shape. She said her people lived near this hill. A few days later, Lewis saw some Shoshone women gathering food. He greeted them with gifts of beads, paints, and tools. Later, when Sacagawea visited the Shoshone camp, she saw the Shoshone chief, Cameahwait, and jumped to her feet. Cameahwait was her brother! Weeping, she ran and threw her arms around him. She had been away from her family for many years. They were happy to have her home. Sacagawea helped Lewis and Clark **barter** for 29 horses and then continued west with the explorers. The Shoshone let Old Toby, a guide, go with the expedition. Old Toby knew about a trail that passed through the Rocky Mountains and he could guide the men along it.

Right: *In 1940, artist N. C. Wyeth painted this picture of Sacagawea traveling with the expedition.*

Below: *A painting by Charles Marion Russell (1865–1926) shows Captain Lewis meeting the Shoshone.*

Right: This picture shows one of the men from the expedition looking at the Rocky Mountains. Left: In December 1805, the explorers built their winter camp, Fort Clatsop. They named the fort after the nearby friendly Native Americans, called the Clatsop.

FORT CLATSOP 1805-06 WINTER QUARTERS of LEWIS AND CLARK EXPEDITION

Over the Mountains and to the Sea

The explorers reached the Rocky Mountains in late August 1805. They had never seen mountains as tall as the Rockies. More mountains lay beyond each ridge. During the hard trip over the mountains, the horses often would tumble down the steep slopes. After a second difficult climb, the explorers crossed the **Continental Divide**, which includes the highest points on the continent. Soon the **climate** turned damp and foggy. When paddling the Columbia River, they thought the water in the river began to taste salty like the ocean. On November 7, 1805, the men paddled through heavy fog and rain. When it cleared, Clark wrote in his **journal**, "Ocean in view. O! The joy!" On November 18, they saw the Pacific Ocean close-up.

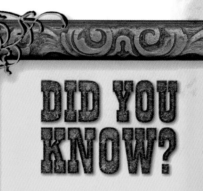

DID YOU KNOW?

After almost 18 months of travel, Clark guessed that they had traveled 4,162 miles (6,698 km) from the mouth of the Missouri to the Pacific Ocean. His figure was within 40 miles (64 km) of the actual amount!

A Risky Return

After spending the winter of 1805–06 at Fort Clatsop, Lewis and Clark packed their boats with supplies for the return trip in March 1806. Wishing to map one more fork of the Columbia River, Lewis and his group headed north for a month. Meanwhile, Clark and his group planned to explore a southern route through Montana. They all would meet again at a place where the Yellowstone River joins the Missouri River.

Now far away from Clark, Lewis faced eight Blackfeet warriors. The Blackfeet were a feared and powerful people. They all decided to camp together for the night. At dawn, a fight broke out. A warrior tried to steal an explorer's rifle. In a struggle, one of Lewis's men stabbed the warrior. Lewis had to shoot another warrior before he and his men could escape.

Above: *Warriors return from a hunt to this Blackfeet village.*

Left: *This 1832 painting by George Catlin shows a Blackfeet medicine man. The Blackfeet were given their name because they dyed their moccasins black.*

Welcomed Heroes

By mid-August 1806, Lewis and Clark reached the Mandan village along the upper Missouri River. They left Sacagawea, Toussaint, and Jean Baptiste there and continued on their return voyage. On September 23, 1806, crowds cheered from the riverbanks in St. Louis, Missouri, welcoming the men home. In all, the **Corps** of Discovery, as the members of the expedition later would be called, traveled and mapped about 8,000 miles (13,000 km) of territory. They described 300 different plants and animals for science. They also described the Native Americans whom they had met. These brave men returned with maps of the growing nation and showed others the way to the West.

A 1954 postage stamp honored the Lewis and Clark expedition. The explorers became heroes for their bravery and success in crossing the continent.

Glossary

barter (BAR-tur) To trade.

burrows (BUR-ohz) Holes animals dig in the ground for shelter.

climate (KLY-mit) The kind of weather a certain area has.

Continental Divide (kon-tin-EN-tul dih-VYD) In North America, it is also called the Great Divide. It is the highest point on the continent, which is in the Rocky Mountains. It divides all of the rivers so that the water on one side of the Divide flows west, toward the Pacific Ocean. The water on the other side flows east, toward the Atlantic Ocean.

Corps (KOR) A group of people working together to reach a certain goal.

divided (di-VY-ded) Separated into two or more parts.

encountered (in-KOWN-terd) Met by chance.

expedition (ek-spuh-DIH-shun) A group of people on a trip for a special purpose, such as scientific study.

explore (ek-SPLOR) To go over carefully or examine.

frontier (frun-TEER) The edge of a settled country, where the wilderness begins.

interpret (in-TER-pret) To explain the meaning of one language with another.

journal (JER-nuhl) A diary or notebook in which people write their thoughts.

militia (muh-LIH-shuh) A group of people who are trained and ready to fight in an emergency.

territory (TEHR-uh-tohr-ee) Land that is controlled by a person or a group of people.

trekked (TRECT) Went on a journey.

Index

C
Charbonneau, Toussaint,
    12, 22
Columbia River, 19, 20
Continental Divide, 19

F
Fort Clatsop, 20
Fort Mandan, 12

G
Great Falls, 15

J
Jean Baptiste, 12, 22
Jefferson, President Thomas,
    4

L
Louisiana Purchase, 4

M
Mandan, 12, 15, 22
Mississippi River, 4
Missouri River, 8, 12, 15,
    22

P
Pacific Ocean, 4, 19
prairie dogs, 8

R
Rocky Mountains, 4, 12,
    16, 19

S
Sacagawea, 12, 16, 22
Shoshone, 12, 16
St. Louis, 8, 22

Web Sites

To learn more about Lewis and Clark's Voyage of Discovery, check out these
Web sites:

www.nationalgeographic.com/west/main.html
www.surfnetkids.com/lewisclark.htm
www.ucds.org/LCWeb/lchome.htm